**PUFFIN**

KNOW-IT-A

# INCREDIBLE CREATURES

If being a writer wasn't Nigel Crowle's full-time job, he'd still be doing it for fun. He's written for children's TV series like "Tweenies", "The Chuckle Brothers" and "Balamory", and for big stars like Ant and Dec, Elton John, Lenny Henry, Caroline Quentin, Donny Osmond, Basil Brush and Jonathan Ross.
He lives in Cardiff with his wife, son and dog where his scripts, plays and books hopefully keep his family:
(a) occupied
(b) amused
(c) in the manner to which they've become accustomed (especially Dexter Dog!)

*Books by Nigel Crowle*

KNOW-IT-ALL GUIDES: CONQUERING ROMANS
KNOW-IT-ALL GUIDES: INCREDIBLE CREATURES

# KNOW-IT-ALL GUIDES

## INCREDIBLE CREATURES

### FAR-OUT FACTS to impress your FRIENDS!

## Nigel Crowle

*Illustrated by Martin Chatterton*

PUFFIN BOOKS

Published by the Penguin Group
Penguin Books Ltd, 80 Strand, London WC2R 0RL, England
Penguin Group (USA) Inc., 375 Hudson Street, New York, New York 10014, USA
Penguin Group (Canada), 90 Eglington Avenue East, Suite 700, Toronto,
Ontario, Canada M4P 2Y3 (a division of Pearson Penguin Canada Inc.)
Penguin Ireland, 25 St Stephen's Green, Dublin 2, Ireland
(a division of Penguin Books Ltd)
Penguin Group (Australia), 250 Camberwell Road, Camberwell, Victoria 3124,
Australia (a division of Pearson Australia Group Pty Ltd)
Penguin Books India Pvt Ltd, 11 Community Centre, Panchsheel Park, New Delhi
– 110 017, India
Penguin Group (NZ), cnr Airborne and Rosedale Roads, Albany, Auckland 1310,
New Zealand (a division of Pearson New Zealand Ltd)
Penguin Books (South Africa) (Pty) Ltd, 24 Sturdee Avenue, Rosebank,
Johannesburg 2196, South Africa

Penguin Books Ltd, Registered Offices: 80 Strand, London WC2R 0RL, England

www.penguin.com

Published 2005
1

Text copyright © Nigel Crowle, 2005
Illustrations copyright © Martin Chatterton, 2005
All rights reserved

The moral right of the author and illustrator has been asserted

Set in Bookman Old Style
Made and printed in England by Clays Ltd, St Ives plc

Except in the United States of America, this book is sold subject to the condition
that it shall not, by way of trade or otherwise, be lent, re-sold, hired out, or otherwise circulated without the publisher's prior consent in any form of binding or
cover other than that in which it is published and without a similar condition
including this condition being imposed on the subsequent purchaser

British Library Cataloguing in Publication Data
A CIP catalogue record for this book is available from the British Library

ISBN-13: 978–0–14131–975–9
ISBN-10: 0–141–31975–5

*It'd be beastly not to dedicate this book to my own two Incredible Creatures: Melanie, my wife, and Siôn, my son. Huge thanks for their support and inspiration, and for always believing in me... whether I've been a dumb bunny or an eager beaver!*

*It's also dedicated to my mum and dad, who've always been proud as peacocks and encouraged me in everything I do, until the cows come home.*

*Animal instincts tell me to give thanks to Jane, my hawk-eyed editor, and to Sarah, my wise owl of an agent, for their invaluable help in making this book appear on the shelves.*

*Also, I've read a huge amount of reference books to gather these facts, so to thank individual authors and bookworms would take longer than this book itself. Nevertheless, when it came to research, I'm grateful to all of them for not sending me on any wild goose chases.*

Look at the top right-hand corner of every page
and you'll see me.
Flick the pages and watch me get my dinner!

# Contents

So, You Want to Know about ...
Weird Creatures?     1

1. Creepy-crawlies     2
2. Under the Water     15
3. Dangerous Animals!     23
4. Down in the Jungle     33
5. Masters of Disguise     38
6. Incredible Journeys     46
7. Record-breaking Birds and Beasts     52
8. Working Animals     64
9. Baby Animals     73
10. Strange but True     79
11. Bird Brains     90
12. Communication Breakdown     98
13. Our Furry Friends     105
14. Find That Fib ... Answers     114

# So, You Want to Know about... Weird Creatures?

Come on . . . admit it!

There are bound to be moments in your life when you wish you could surprise your parents, dumbfound your teacher, or impress that rich auntie – the one who insists upon doling out pocket money the moment she hears an amazing fact.

So, how do you learn all that impressive stuff without wasting your life for years and years because you've spent all your free time swotting up?

Well, the answer's simple – all you have to do is . . . Read This Book!

It will tell you everything you need to know about weird creatures . . . and then some!

So, flick through the following, and learn all sorts of gob-smackingly unbelievable yet true stuff you never knew you never knew about creepy-crawlies, wild animals, rare breeds and the like.

A word of warning, though – every chapter, you'll find a fact that is complete tosh . . . an out-and-out lie. A load of balderdash, in fact!

Can you Find That Fib among these fabulously and fantastically fascinating facts?

Read on, dear reader . . .

# 1. Creepy-crawlies

**Let's begin with a quick look at the creatures biologists and scientists refer to as 'mini-beasts' – and that we normal human beings call 'something small and horrible that scares us by scuttling behind the curtains'. Oh, and don't forget to Find That Fib!**

## Cockroach Capers

Do we human beings have anything at all in common with cockroaches? Well, we're both omnivores, meaning that we eat anything organic – but cockroaches are known to eat some disgusting stuff.

**Top Eight Cockroach Meals (in order of yuckiness):**
8. Postage stamp glue
7. Paper
6. Paint
5 Grease
4. Shoe polish
3. Sweat
2. Human toenails
1. Fellow cockroaches

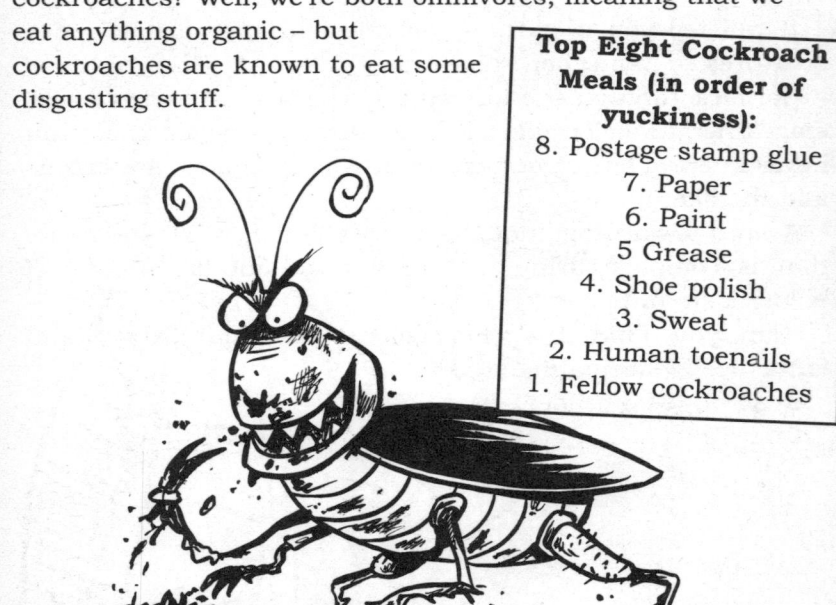

But there is one other major difference between humans and humble cockroaches. If you chop off a cockroach's head, it can still live, quite happily, for a whole week!

In 2001, Australian freestyle aerial skier Jacqui Cooper surprised surgeons with the speed of her recovery from a fractured backbone. She insisted that this was due to drinking a yucky cocktail of Diet Coke mixed with . . . crushed cockroaches!

**Best Use of Cockroaches**

The average flea is about 3 millimetres long, yet it can jump over 30 centimetres – which is about 100 times its own length. If humans could do the same, it'd be like someone jumping more than three times the height of Nelson's Column in London's Trafalgar Square . . . and do it from a standing start!

Speaking of defying gravity, spiders can hang around the smoothest of surfaces with the help of minute hairs on all eight of their feet. These 624,000 setules (tiny hairs on the ends of hairs) generate an adhesive force strong enough to hold 173 times the spider's own weight. As one scientist put it, 'That's like Spiderman clinging to a building by his fingertips and toes while rescuing 173 adults who are hanging on to his back.'

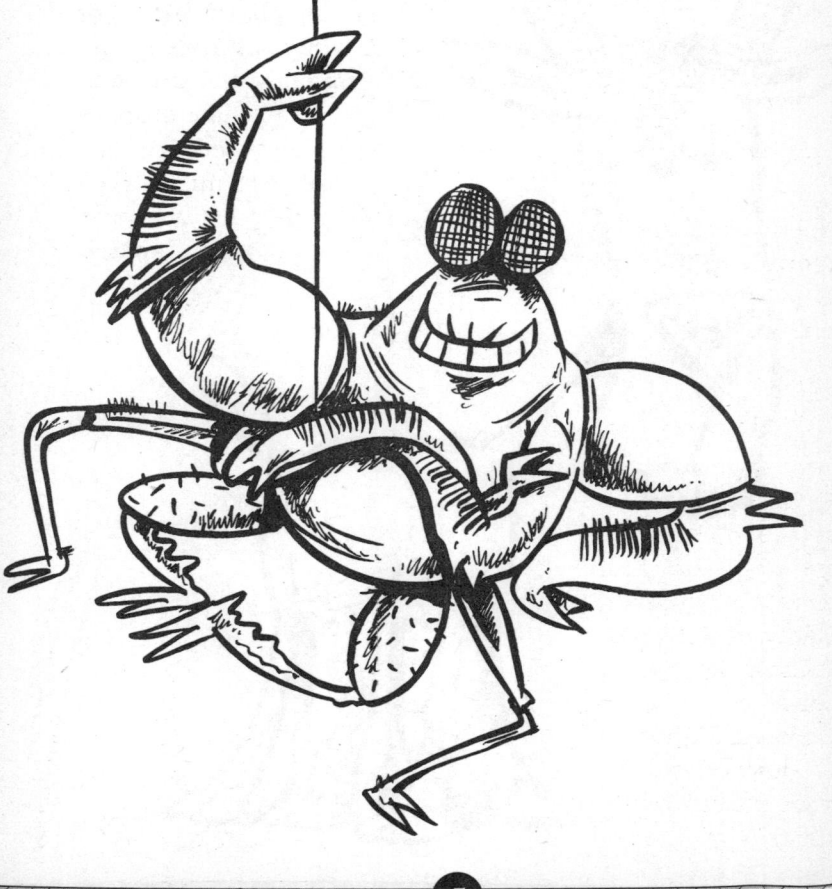

Not only are spiders super-strong, their webs are actually five times as strong as steel. A strand of spiderweb can be stretched by 31 per cent without breaking; it's finer than a human hair, and it's lighter than cotton. In fact, it is the perfect material to make bullet-proof vests, or the cables that hold up suspension bridges. And this is why scientists in Quebec have created spider silk substitute using goats' milk. Not only will they get as much of the precious silk-like stuff as they need, it's also easier to milk a goat than squirt it from a spider.

Midges have the fastest wingbeat on record – being able to flap over 1,046 times a second.

The bombardier beetle uses chemical warfare to defeat its enemies. When attacked, it fires a cloud of disgusting brown gas out of its bottom. This blinds any attackers – who have already been scared stiff by the cracking sound the explosion makes as the chemicals mix. It blows out the gas in rapid squirts, a bit like the rat-a-tat of a machine gun. If it fired the gas in one long burst of spray, it would be such a hot and powerful blast, it would blow the bombardier beetle's bottom off! Flip to the front cover to see the bombardier beetle in action.

Humans can carry around their own creepy-crawlies without knowing it. Never eat undercooked or raw pork or beef or fish – infected portions can contain tapeworms – or else *you* could contain a tapeworm, too! Tapeworms are yucky creatures: parasites that grip on to our intestines and eat away inside our stomachs until (in some cases) they:
**a)** grow over 9 metres in length
**b)** go on a crash diet
**c)** get bored and eat themselves.

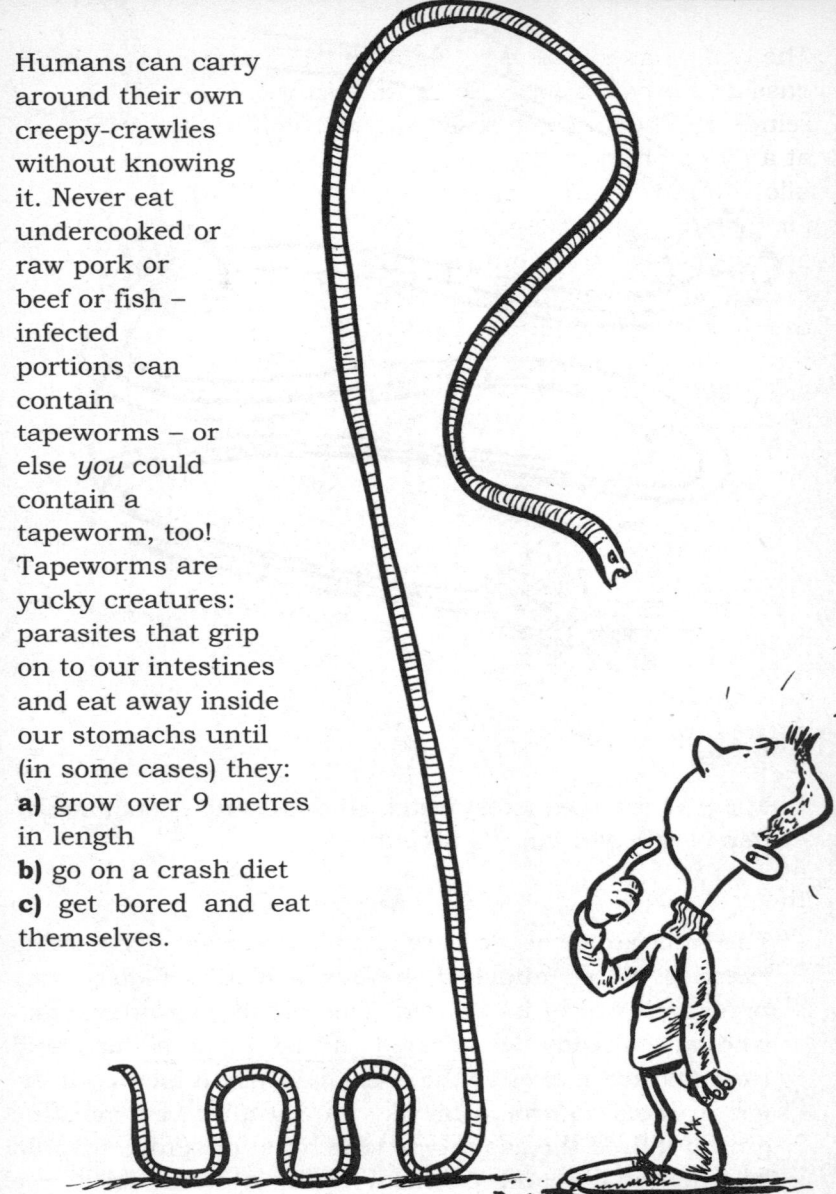

*The answer is: a) they can grow to over 9 metres in length, almost the length of two estate cars.*

The botfly has a disgusting habit. It waits for a passing caribou (a large North American reindeer). Then it zooms into the caribou's face at a speed of up to 30 kilometres an hour, aiming for the animal's moist upper lip. The botfly sprays out its maggot brood, hoping that they'll land either there or up the caribou's nostrils. From either landing spot,

the maggots then crawl along the roof of the caribou's mouth and end up in the caribou's nasal passage, which makes a perfect breeding ground. Disgusting!

Watch out when a huge column of large-jawed army ants goes on the march through a forest. If something gets in their way, they either attack it – or eat it! Not even a forest fire will stop them – the mass of ants simply swarm into it and put the fire out by suffocating it with their own bodies.

# Top Four Names for Woodlice
(in order of weirdness)

**4.** in Hirwaun in Wales, they're called 'Granny Greys'
**3.** in Kent, they're known as 'Monkey-peas'
**2.** in Devon, they're known as 'God's pigs'
**1.** in Lancashire, they call them 'Fairies' hogs'.

In the nineteenth century, woodlice were swallowed as pills:
**a)** by humans to cure tuberculosis
**b)** by cows to cure hairballs
**c)** by athletes to cure athlete's foot.

## Other strange names for woodlice include:

Bibble-bugs
Sow-bugs
Cud-worms
Tiggy-hogs
Shoe-laces
Sink-lice
Slaters
Coffin cutters
Cheesy-bites

*The answer is both a) and b). Those nutty Victorians also suggested making woodlice into a tasty sauce.*

Nasutus soldier termites are actually blind. However, if they're attacked by larger ants, they squirt a glue-like substance at them through tubes at the front of their heads. The antennae and legs of their enemies get all tangled in the gooey thread that first paralyses, then chokes them.

Most microbes are so tiny, you can't see them without a microscope or magnifying glass. However, *Thiomargarita namibiensis* is a giant single-celled bacterium found on the ocean floor off the African coast. It grows to almost a millimetre in diameter – the size of the full stop at the end of this sentence. (Yes, that one back there.)

Scientists in the USA believe they've made an incredible breakthrough to stop annoying mosquitoes sucking blood. They've created an aerosol spray which actually turns a mosquito's stomach at the taste of blood. Instead, the insect survives by slurping away at sugar supplies in soft drinks like cola or lemonade.

The black widow spider may have a fearsome name, but in reality this deadly insect is a bit of a wuss! Black widows hate light, so when we disturb them they attack because they are frightened. Don't point and laugh for too long, though, as females can inject enough poison to kill a human.

The word 'caterpillar' comes from the old Latin words for 'cat' and 'hair'. So, I suppose our ancestors must have thought that caterpillars looked a bit like small furry kittens!

### Top Nine British Beetle Names (in order of oddness):

9. Churchyard
8. Museum
7. Bloody-Nosed
6. Pink Jewel
5. Oil
4. Bacon
3. Thistle Tortoise
2. Turnip Flea
1. Boat-shaped Fungus

# 2. Under the Water

**Next time you're taking a dip in the sea, or dangling your toes in the river . . . watch out. Not everything underwater is as harmless as a dopey, gulping goldfish from a funfair! And don't forget to Find That Fib!**

Caviar may look like tiny black marbles covered in slime, but apparently it tastes delicious. As one of the world's most expensive foods, caviar is the name given to the eggs of the sturgeon, a huge fish that can grow up to five metres in length. Sturgeon – which can live for 150 years – have remained almost unchanged since prehistoric times. The beluga sturgeon, found in the seas off the coast of Russia, produces the most prized caviar, which can cost more than £1,200 a pound (450 grams).

Despite the natural colour of the common goldfish, it isn't really orange. Photoelectric cells buried just below a goldfish's skin react to the smallest amount of sunlight, giving the impression that the goldfish is actually bright orange in colour.

And so, what colour is a goldfish really?
a) ghostly white
b) yellowy-green
c) blue-grey

*The answer's b) – goldfish are really a sickly yellowy-green!*

Whales, dolphins and porpoises belong to a family of mammals called cetaceans. They are all warm-blooded, feed their young with milk, and live their lives in water. Even though they're related, their sizes make it easy to tell a blue whale from a common dolphin. A female blue whale's heart can weigh 10 times as much as an average dolphin! However, it's not so easy to tell a dolphin and a porpoise apart . . . unless, of course, you flip over the page for our handy guide!

# Differences Between a Dolphin and a Porpoise:

### Dolphin
Protruding snout or beak
Grows up to 3 metres
Tall, curved dorsal fin on its back
Cone-shaped teeth
Can live up to 50 years

### Porpoise
Smaller, rounded body shape
Grows up to 2 metres
Fast swimmer
Shy
Spade-shaped teeth
Can live up to 20 years

When you catch a gurnard fish and take it out of the water, it starts grunting at you – well, you would, wouldn't you? Some say this gave the gurnard its name – coming from the French word for 'grumbler'.

'Some days I wish I'd stayed in my sea-bed...'

Looking for the perfect pet for your annoying brother or irritating sister? Why not give them a large mantis shrimp? Growing up to 25 centimetres long, a large shrimp can easily smash through the double-layered safety glass of an aquarium.

This punchy crustacean is also known as the boxer shrimp because it uses its heavily calcified front leg as a club to shatter the hard shells of its prey with the impact of a .22-calibre bullet. This 'punch' is not only quick – going from rest to 10 metres per second in 4–8 milliseconds (50 times faster than we blink our eyes) – it also packs quite a force, reaching well over 100 times the mantis shrimp's body weight.

Here's a shocking fact. The electric eel isn't an eel – it's a freshwater fish with a really long body. It grows up to 2.5 metres long, with most of that length being tail. It makes electricity from muscles in its body, and it uses this power to zap and kill unsuspecting fishes. Any disturbance to this force field alerts it to the arrival of an unsuspecting fish – or human! These generating cells produce a series of brief shocks which add up to around 650 volts. If discharged at once, that would be enough to stun a donkey . . . although if a donkey were daft enough to be underwater with electric eels around, then it deserves all it gets!

'A donkey swimming? What's shocking about that?'

'Look! I'm a Plat-Billed Ducky Puss!'

**Most Mixed-up Mammal**

Australia's duck-billed platypus is one mixed-up mammal! It has a beak like a duck, a tail like a beaver, lays eggs like birds and reptiles, yet suckles its young like mammals. When a stuffed duck-billed platypus was sent to England in 1797, scientists were convinced it was a joke. They couldn't believe that such an animal actually existed!

Sperm whales have the largest brains of any living animal species. Some male whales have brains that weigh as much as 9.2 kilograms, which is almost 6 times larger than our human brains.

# Top Three Weird Yet Attractive-sounding Names for Sea-slugs:

3.
Pyjama Nudibranch

2.
Flamingo-Tongue Snail

1.
Haitian Jewel Snail

# 3. Dangerous Animals!

Read this next bit very carefully. You never know when these facts will help you. At the very least, you'll discover that it's not exactly a clever idea to offer to brush a puma's teeth... so, don't do it! Try to Find That Fib, instead!

Stay away from a bull elephant when it's in a state called '*musth*' – that's when it behaves extremely dangerously as its body is producing an excess of male hormones. They ooze with a disgusting smell from glands on the forehead, and the elephant will attack anything and everything. No one knows exactly why this happens . . . probably because no one dares risk death by getting close. So, remember, you *mustn't* approach an elephant in *musth*!

Surfers off the west coast of Wales have taken to wearing silk pyjamas instead of wetsuits. They don't do this for fashion purposes, or to keep out the cold. They do it to combat the deadly attentions of the box jellyfish.

It seems that the individual stinging cells that make the box jellyfish's sting so dangerous and painful are easily able to slip between the fibres used in constructing an ordinary wetsuit. However, they can't penetrate the more dense fibre layer of silk PJs.

**Weirdest Fashion**

# The 22 Remaining Croc and Gator Varieties in the World

African slender-snouted crocodile
American alligator
American crocodile
Black caiman alligator
Broad-snouted caiman
Chinese alligator
Common caiman
Cuban crocodile
Cuvier's dwarf caiman
Dwarf crocodile
False gharial
Gharial
Indo-Pacific crocodile
Johnston's crocodile
Morelet's crocodile
Mugger crocodile
New Guinea crocodile
Nile crocodile
Orinoco crocodile
Philippine crocodile
Schneider's dwarf caiman
Siamese crocodile
(By the way, a caiman is just a fancy name for a crocodile.)

100 million years ago, crocs and gators ruled the earth. Now, many species are in danger of becoming extinct.

*Never smile at a crocodile. Or an alligator!*

## Crocodiles vs Alligators

Do you want to know what makes a crocodile different from an alligator? Well, don't peer too closely at either a croc or a gator – it's much safer to use this Handy Three-part Guide instead:

1.
**Crocodiles** have glands on their tongues which allow them to get rid of excess salt. Unlike alligators, crocodiles can live happily in salt water.
2.
**Alligators** have wide, U-shaped noses like spades which help to crack open shelled animals like turtles and hard-shelled invertebrates. Crocodiles have longer, more pointed, V-shaped noses, ideal for a wide variety of prey.
3.
**Alligators** have a wider upper jaw which almost completely overlaps their lower jaw and hides their bottom teeth. Crocodiles have upper and lower jaws the same size, and their teeth interlock when their jaws snap shut.

When a blackbird is attacked by a hawk, the alarm call it makes to warn fellow blackbirds sounds similar to:
**a)** the noise you make when you stub your toe
**b)** a car alarm going off
**c)** someone yelling the word 'hawk'.

Funnel web spiders are the sort of Australian beasties you don't want to mess with if you're Down Under. Humans and monkeys are extremely sensitive to funnel web spider venom. However, household pets, such as mice, rabbits, guinea pigs, dogs and cats, seem to have excellent immune systems and can survive 100 times as much spider venom as it'd take to kill a human being.

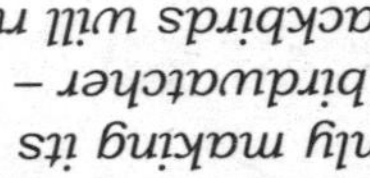

*The answer is c), but the blackbird's only making its usual short distress cry, which – to a slightly deaf birdwatcher – might sound like it's yelling 'Hawk!' Other blackbirds will rush for cover.*

## Worst Breath

Only two species of lizard – the Gila monster and the Mexican beaded lizard – are poisonous. This venom runs down grooves in their teeth as they bite into a victim's flesh. It was thought that the Gila monster had such poisonously bad breath that one whiff was enough to make its prey keel over, curl up and die! That's not true, although if you do snack on rotting flesh, then your breath won't exactly smell minty fresh!

# Animals that Fish for Food:

- The hairy imperial spider hangs from a horizontal thread and lowers another thread with a sticky drop on its end, which it swings round in a circle. Curious male moths (its only prey) are attracted by a false scent the spider also spreads in the night air. They fly closer and get stuck on the sticky silk ball or bola. They're then caught – hook, line and sinker!

- The anglerfish lies in wait for a fishy food morsel to swim past, then waggles a spine on its head which looks like a fishing rod. This has a fleshy tip which resembles a worm. It rapidly swings back its lure before swallowing its prey – otherwise it'd be swallowing a bit of itself . . . which would be painful!

- Temminck's snapper or alligator snapping turtle is the world's largest freshwater turtle, growing up to 110 kilograms. It lies on a river bed with its mouth open and wiggles a pink, worm-like growth on its tongue to trap unsuspecting prey such as fish, frogs, snakes, snails and even other turtles!

# The world's Five Most Poisonous Snakes:

**5.**
**Tiger snake:** this nasty reptile kills more people in Australia than any other.

**4.**
**Taipan:** venom delivered in a single Taipan bite can kill up to 12,000 guinea pigs.

**3.**
**Krait:** 50 per cent of the bites from this Asian snake are fatal.

**2.**
**Australian brown snake:** 0.00203 of a millilitre of its venom is enough to kill a person.

**1.**
**Fierce snake or Inland taipan:**
takes the top spot, with the deadliest venom of any snake! One bite from this Aussie killer's huge fangs is enough to kill over 250,000 mice – that's 100 people!

# Hippo's Hitlist

How can you tell if a hippopotamus has taken a dislike to you? With this simple guide, it's easy!

**1.**
He's vocal – making a grumpy, bellowing sound.
**2.**
Then he yawns.
**3.**
Then he blows bubbles underwater.
**4.**
Then he jumps up and snaps at the water.
**5.**
Then *you* get out of the water, double quick!

# 4. Down in the Jungle

It's night . . . it's pitch-black . . . and you're in a hammock in the middle of the jungle.

You can't sleep, because you're trying to work out what sort of creature makes a blood-curdling noise like 'Oohh...ohhh...aggg... agggh...yearghhhhhhh!' Don't worry, just stay awake and try to Find That Fib among the following facts.

You may have been told that if you're ever unlucky enough to be chased by a crocodile, run in a zigzag motion – because crocs can't change direction easily! Actually, this isn't true. It's safer to run in a straight line to escape because humans, who can run as fast as 30 kilometres per hour, will always outrun a crocodile, which only reaches a lumbering 12–14 kilometres per hour. However, don't let them get too close as they can capture prey by lunging forward at 12 metres per second!

**Most Useful Croc Tip**

*Hmm, must nip down the waterhole and buy some more nappies...*

Rhino horns are made of the same protein substance (called keratin) that makes up our human hair and nails.

The square-lipped white rhino is not actually white in colour. It was named after the explorer who first discovered it in 1805, Sir Francis Clifford White. The female of the species is such a fast breeder that she can give birth to over 15 babies at a time and does so, on average, every 2–3 months which – in summer months – leads to breeding grounds becoming overrun with rhinos.

Hollywood may be a long way from the jungle, but some stars still have a close connection. High-kicking, back-flipping, bone-crunching Jackie Chan, kung-fu's most famous movie star, is also an international ambassador for the protection of endangered animals. Jackie was alarmed by the fact that there are fewer than 7,000 wild tigers left in Asia. That's why the kung-fu king has put his name to a conservation campaign to stop the illegal trade in wildlife.

'At risk' species that Jackie Chan wants to protect include:

**Tiger:** hunted for its skin and bones
**Sea turtle:** hunted for its shell
**Indian one-horned rhino:** hunted for its horn
**Asian elephant:** hunted for its ivory tusks
**Musk deer:** hunted to make perfume from its glands
**Sloth bear:** hunted for its gall bladder and paws.

## Six Elephant Jokes

1. Each night, elephants make pillows to lie on when they go to sleep.
2. Elephants can sniff water from five kilometres away.
3. They have no bones in their trunks, which can hold up to four litres of water.
4. Using their trunks, elephants can pick a pin off the ground, untie a slip knot, or pull the trigger of a gun.

   In the 1880s, the Duke of Devonshire's pet elephant could supposedly uncork a bottle of wine.
5. An elephant's knee joints are much lower down than in hoofed animals – which is why it can bend its hind legs like a human kneeling.
6. Elephants have a kind of shock absorber in their feet. It's a fatty tissue that allows them to muffle noises – like sticks cracking – as they quietly walk along.

# Three Differences Between African and Asian Elephants:

1. **The African elephant has two fingers on the tip of its trunk, which it uses to grab things. The Asian elephant only has one finger, which it uses as a scoop.**

2. **The Asian elephant has two humps on its forehead, while its African cousin's is smooth.**

3. **The African elephant's ears are at least three times the size of the Asian elephant's. Each elephant's ear is unique and is used as a type of fingerprint for identification.**

# 5. Masters of Disguise

**There are moments in life when you wish you could just disappear, blending into the background.**

**For instance, when you've accidentally spilt curry sauce on the new sofa. You might need a camouflage fact to defuse the situation. If so, read on . . . Oh, and don't forget to Find That Fib!**

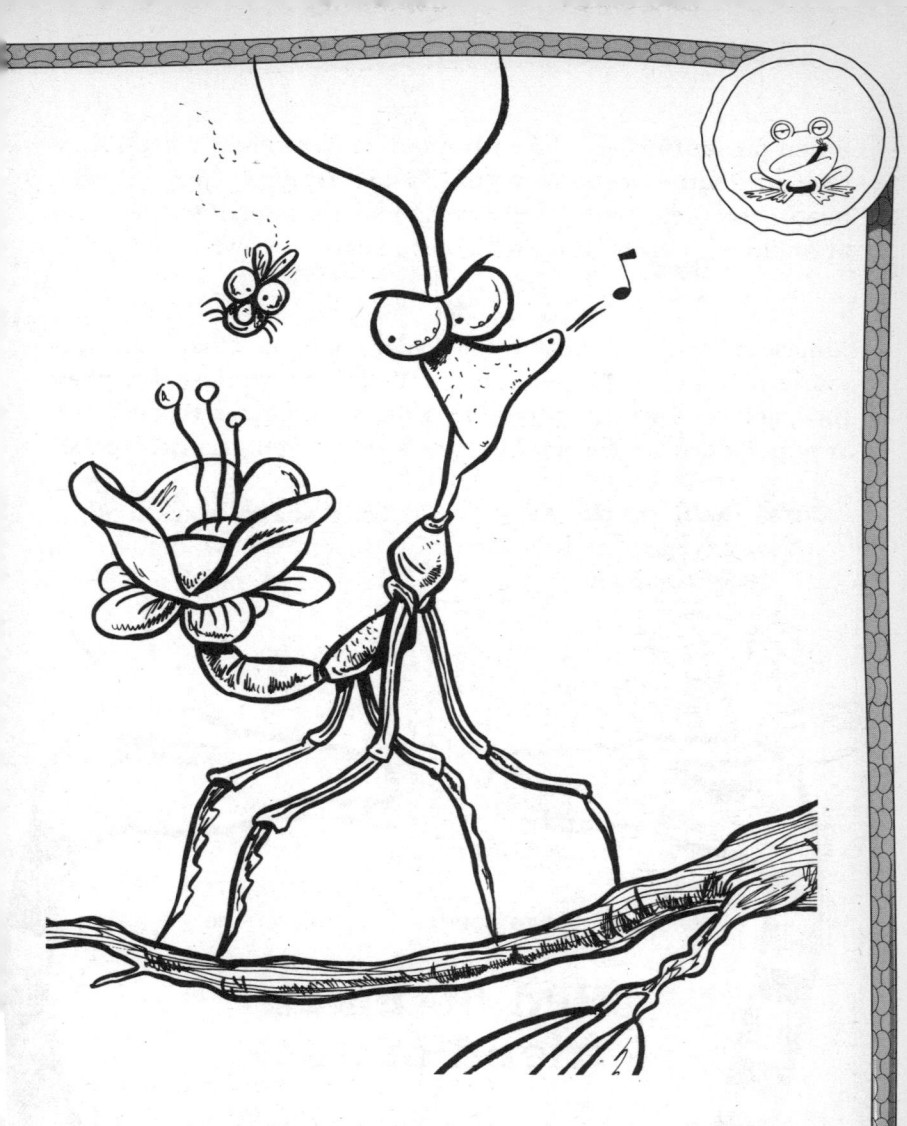

The African devil's flower mantis hangs from a branch, pretending to be a brightly coloured flower. Most of this insect's body is coloured green like a leaf stem, apart from its bottom, which it turns to look like a red bloom! The mantis watches over its shoulder as an insect homes in on the 'lovely flower', then swings round at the last moment and snaps it up.

When owl butterflies of South America close their wings, they reveal a feathered pattern that looks strangely like an owl's head, complete with large eyespots. This terrifies possible attackers – mainly birds which are scared of owls.

American king snakes aren't poisonous, and so they are vulnerable to hunting mammals. To protect themselves, they have coloured warning band markings, similar to those of the very poisonous coral snake. Here's how to tell the difference:

**Coral snake markings:**
black, yellow, red, yellow, black

**King snake markings:**
black, yellow, black, red, black

Or, to put it in good ol' US folk rhyme:

## 'Red 'n' black – friend of Jack.

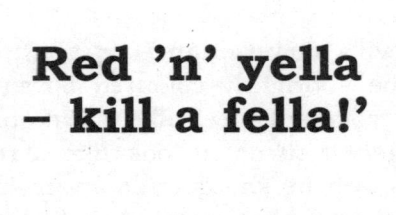

## Red 'n' yella – kill a fella!'

**Most Moody Animal**

We all know that chameleons can change colour from brown, green, blue, yellow, red and black, to white. However, the reason why they do it is not to camouflage themselves – it's to tell other creatures how they're feeling. Angry chameleons turn yellow, whereas a much cooler, calmer chameleon goes green.

The *Papilio aegeus* butterfly has a clever way of dealing with unwelcome hunters. Knowing that bird droppings are quite common on leaves and vegetation, the caterpillar makes itself look as much like bird droppings as possible: a disgusting mix of white splattered on brown!

The octopus is the real star of the camouflage world. It uses pigment-filled sacs (called 'chromataphores') just beneath its skin to change colour and texture. By doing this, it can blend into the background against sand, pebbles, reef rubble, seaweeds and even bright spiked corals. As a back-up defence system, it can also squirt black, red or brown pigment from an ink sac to form a smokescreen which clouds several cubic metres of water and creates a highly effective means of escape for the octopus.

South America's Suriname toad is the world's flattest amphibian. Side-on, it measures only about 20 millimetres wide and it looks like the poor creature has been well and truly stamped on! It is a greyish brown colour and looks like a dead floating leaf as it lies in murky water. That's exactly what it wants fish to think – when they get too close, the Suriname toad lunges forward and grabs a meal!

**Flattest Toad**

Two close relatives of the sea horse, the leafy sea dragon and the weedy sea dragon, have very appropriate names. They both look like:
a) fronds of exotically coloured seaweed
b) vegetarian dishes you wouldn't touch in a Chinese restaurant
c) Plants you would find in your garden.

*The answer is a) they look like undersea plants. Sea Dragons, however, don't have the gripping tails of their relative, the seahorse.*

We may think that striped zebras look pretty distinctive, but to a lion stalking them for his supper the zebra's long, vertical stripes look like long, vertical grass stems. What's that you say? Zebras have black or brown stripes, while grass is green? You're right – but a lion happens to be colour-blind, so he or she just sees the stripes . . . and not the tasty zebra hiding!

The tiny Cinderella butterfly caterpillar scares off hungry attackers by changing itself into a huge, poisonous-looking spider. When threatened, it changes colour from a sandy brown to bright purple with huge green spots. To top off the transformation, it swells a series of hairy whiskers along its body, making the caterpillar look as if it has eight enormous spider legs.

# 6. Incredible Journeys

**For some of us, it's enough of an effort to get out of bed in the school holidays. In the animal kingdom, however, they're used to travelling much further. Just don't forget to Find That Fib amongst these far-travelled facts.**

Beswick's swans – which breed on the Russian tundra – are very predictable when it comes to migrating. Swans in the west always winter in the Netherlands or the UK, while more easterly swans head for China. Not only do they navigate the same route during their end-of-summer migration, they often arrive on the same date as the year before.

Some seabirds get so used to flying over oceans that they only land to breed. The mighty wandering albatross spends 70 per cent of its life in the air, using winds to help it soar. During breeding, the wandering albatross may travel more than 30,000 kilometres, including trips to find food which can cover hundreds of kilometres.

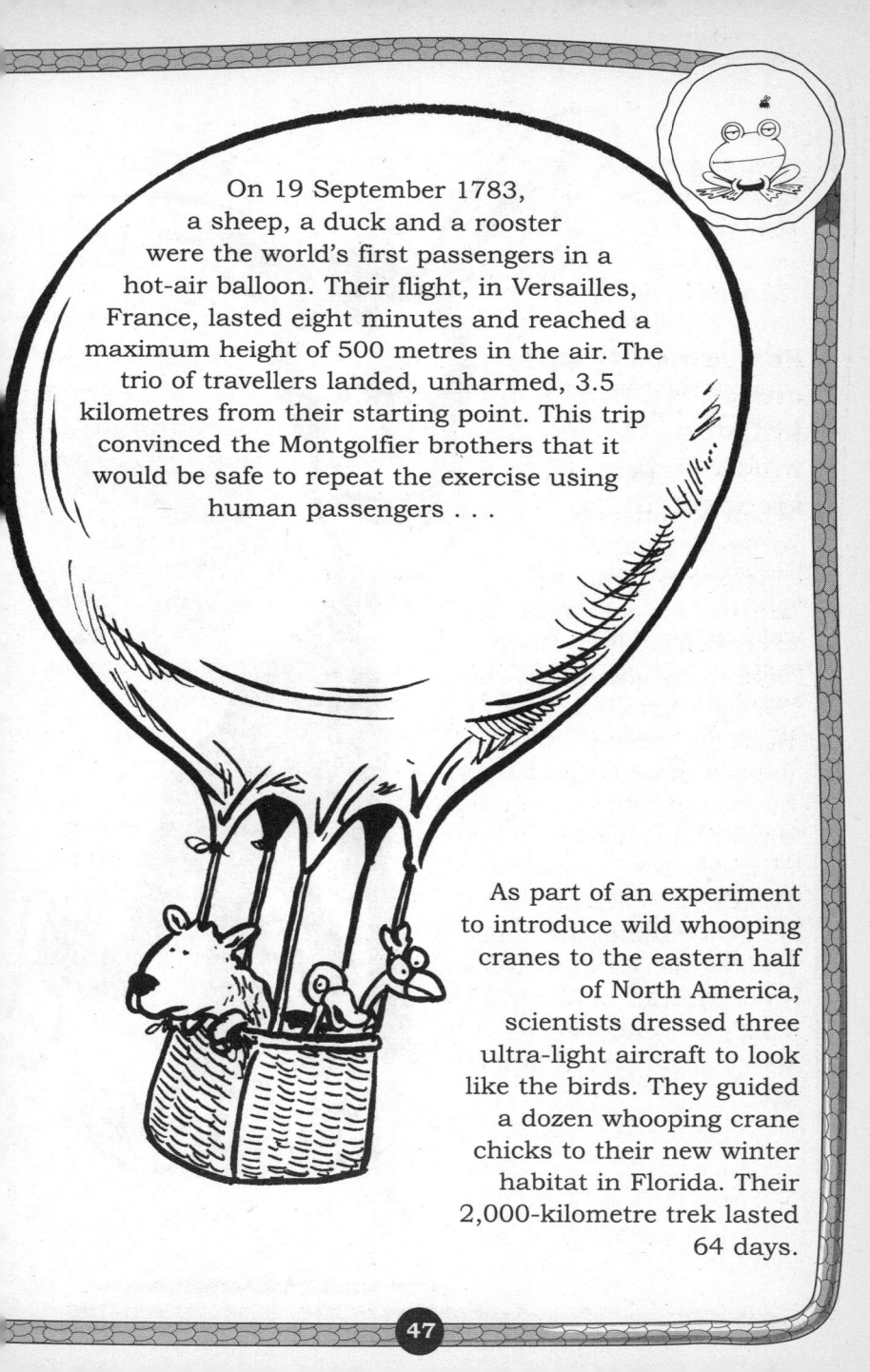

On 19 September 1783, a sheep, a duck and a rooster were the world's first passengers in a hot-air balloon. Their flight, in Versailles, France, lasted eight minutes and reached a maximum height of 500 metres in the air. The trio of travellers landed, unharmed, 3.5 kilometres from their starting point. This trip convinced the Montgolfier brothers that it would be safe to repeat the exercise using human passengers . . .

As part of an experiment to introduce wild whooping cranes to the eastern half of North America, scientists dressed three ultra-light aircraft to look like the birds. They guided a dozen whooping crane chicks to their new winter habitat in Florida. Their 2,000-kilometre trek lasted 64 days.

Camels have three eyelids which they use to protect themselves from irritating grains of swirling sand as they journey across the deserts of the world.

When scientists in Africa nicknamed a chimpanzee 'Dumbo' because his ears were exceptionally large, they were easily able to spot him among other chimps. However, when Dumbo flapped those large ears as he swung from tree to tree, it gave him an extra burst of speed. This meant that Dumbo travelled far more quickly through the jungle – and avoided more predators – than his fellow chimps. That's one chimpanzee who's anything but dumb, eh?

Largest-eared Chimp

Grey whales make one of the longest migration trips of any mammal, travelling distances of up to 22,500 kilometres from summers in the Arctic, so that they can winter in the warm waters off the Mexican coast, where they mate and bear their young. Travelling along the sea bed, the grey whale turns on its side and gulps in huge mouthfuls of silt. It strains out the water and mud, and swallows any bottom-dwelling creatures left behind.

If you've ever looked up on a summer's day and spotted a bird of prey, floating above you and using hot-air currents to soar in the skies, then you'll be aware that these raptors know how to travel. The peregrine falcon, for instance, lives on every continent, except Antarctica.

However, do you know what a peregrine falcon's name really means? Is it:
**a)** 'wanderer'
**b)** 'feathery thing that flies'
**c)** 'melanie'.

*The answer's a), of course—given their flying habits, it's not surprising that they're the 'wanderers' of the bird world.*

Even plastic animals need a change of scenery. In January 1992, 29,000 bathroom toys, turtles, ducks, beavers and frogs, went overboard in the middle of the Pacific Ocean. Pushed by winds and currents, the toys were iced up in Alaska. After taking six years to thaw out and reach the North Atlantic, ducks began to appear off the American coast. The manufacturers of these animal adventurers weren't surprised they'd survived. The toys were designed to withstand a typical toddler's bath-time, and they'd already found that 'little babies can be very rough'.

In midwinter, emperor penguins use their tummies to toboggan their way across 80 kilometres of ice to feast on squid, krill and fish in the Weddell Sea. They have an average cruising speed of one kilometre per hour.

## Biggest Family

The world's population of Mexican free-tailed bats is one big happy family. As many as 50 million of them have been seen emerging from a series of caves in Texas. The entire colony can fly as high as 3,000 metres – that's over 12 times as high as the UK's tallest building, in Canary Wharf, London. No wonder the aircraft controller who picked them up on his radar screen thought he was going batty!

Scientists have discovered how birds migrate over large distances at night without getting lost. They've found that a bird's eye contains cells which can actually register the earth's magnetic field – even if it's dark. Our clever feathered friends then navigate their journeys in the same way that we use a compass.

# 7. Record-breaking Birds and Beasts

Some people say that 'big is beautiful', while others reckon that 'good things come in small packages'. Either way, sometimes, size really is everything – especially if you're trying to break records in the animal kingdom. Check out the following fab facts, but watch out for a big lie as you Find That Fib!

## Widest Wingspan

The wandering albatross has the longest wingspan of any bird, measuring up to 3.6 metres . . .

# Largest Animal

The blue whale is not only the world's largest animal, it's also the largest animal the world has ever known – growing up to 200 tonnes and dwarfing the largest dinosaurs. In 1947 Southern Ocean sailors caught a female blue whale weighing a whopping 190 tonnes. Her heart weighed almost 700 kilograms, and her tongue weighed 4.2 tonnes.

# Largest Eyes

The giant squid's eyes are the largest in the animal kingdom and grow to 25 centimetres in diameter – which is bigger than a dinner plate! Giant squid can grow up to 18 metres in length.

# Largest Egg

The female kiwi lays the largest egg in relation to body size. A kiwi weighs 1.8 kilograms (about the size of a chicken) and it lays an egg weighing 0.45 kilograms and measuring up to 13 centimetres – three times the size of a hen's egg. Not surprising, then, that the kiwi lays just the one egg at a time!

The much heavier ostrich lays an egg 2,000 times the size of the smallest egg, which is laid by the hummingbird. Ostrich eggs weigh about 1.2 kilograms and measure up to 18 centimetres. The eggs themselves take two hours to boil. The ostrich egg is the largest egg laid by any living creature, and is the same in content as 24 hen's eggs.

But how long does an ostrich egg take to boil? Is it:

**a)** one and a half hours
**b)** five weeks
**c)** three years.

*The answer's a)... although good luck to you on finding bread soldiers big enough for an ostrich egg.*

# Longest Flippers

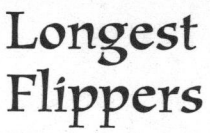

The humpback whale has the longest flippers of any whale, measuring up to 4.3 metres long. They're used to propel these massive creatures – which weigh almost 30 tonnes – completely out of the water.

# Longest Tongue

The giraffe has an unusually long tongue. Coloured pink and black, the tongue can be 56 centimetres long and is used to pluck food from trees.

# The Top Three Fastest Flying Birds:

1. Peregrine falcon: speeds of up to 280 kilometres per hour
2. Spine-tailed swift: speeds of up to 170 kmph
3. Frigate bird: speeds of up to 150 kmph.

# Longest Nose (on a Primate!)

Borneo's proboscis monkey has a huge nose that grows up to 17.5 centimetres long, which is almost a quarter of the monkey's total body length. Now that's a record not to be sniffed at.

# Largest Insect

The mammoth dragonfly of the Amazonian rainforest has a head that is as heavy as a cricket ball. Even the body of this huge insect can weigh as much as 200 grams, and this insect is rarely able to fly distances of more than 12 metres. In fact, many frequently die in mid-air because flapping their wings puts such a strain upon their breathing systems.

# Laziest Animal

The laziest animal in the world has to be the three-toed sloth of South America. It spends 21 of the 24 hours in a day asleep in tree branches, camouflaged as dead leaves. For the mere three hours when it's awake, the sloth is such a slow mover that it swims faster than it walks.

# Fastest Animal

The cheetah – the world's fastest land animal – can reach speeds of up to 100 kmph. What's more, it can reach that speed in just three seconds from an 'On your marks...Get set...Go!'

# Smallest Mammal

The world's smallest non-flying mammal is the tiny Savi's pygmy shrew. It weighs less than 2 grams and is barely 35 millimetres long.

'Peter the 121st, Robert the 79th, Sally the 320th, and Madeline the 130th, will you behave!'

# Fastest Breeder

You won't find a quicker breeder among the many different types of mammals than the American opossum. After becoming pregnant, it gives birth after just 8–13 days. It produces two litters of up to 25 infants, all born naked and blind. The mother licks a path for the babies across her fur – or she may even carry some of them in her mouth. That's probably how the myth of the opossum giving birth to babies through her nose sprung up.

# Largest Living Bird

The flightless ostrich reaches heights of up to 2.75 metres, and weighs up to 157 kilograms. Despite its heaviness, an ostrich can still run at speeds of up to 70 kmph, which is faster than a pursuing lion, leopard or hyena. If it stops, however, and takes a well-aimed kick at, say, that lion, it would probably kill it!

**Best Runner**

'Are you saying I'm *not* the largest living bird? Well? Are you?'

SIZE COMPARISON CHART
(We know it's not quite accurate, but you get the point!)

# Smallest Living Bird

The bee hummingbird is only 6–8 centimetres long – and some of that length is made up of beak. It weighs only 2 grams. Its heart beats 1,000 times a minute and that's when it's resting!

# Top Four Largest Fish

**4. Greenland shark:** 6.5 metres long
**3. Great white shark:** 6 – 8 metres long
**2. Basking shark:** 10 metres long
**1. Whale shark:** 12 – 18 metres long

# Four Differences Between Sharks and Fish

Although sharks are related to fish, they're not mammals like whales. However, sharks aren't like many bony fish.

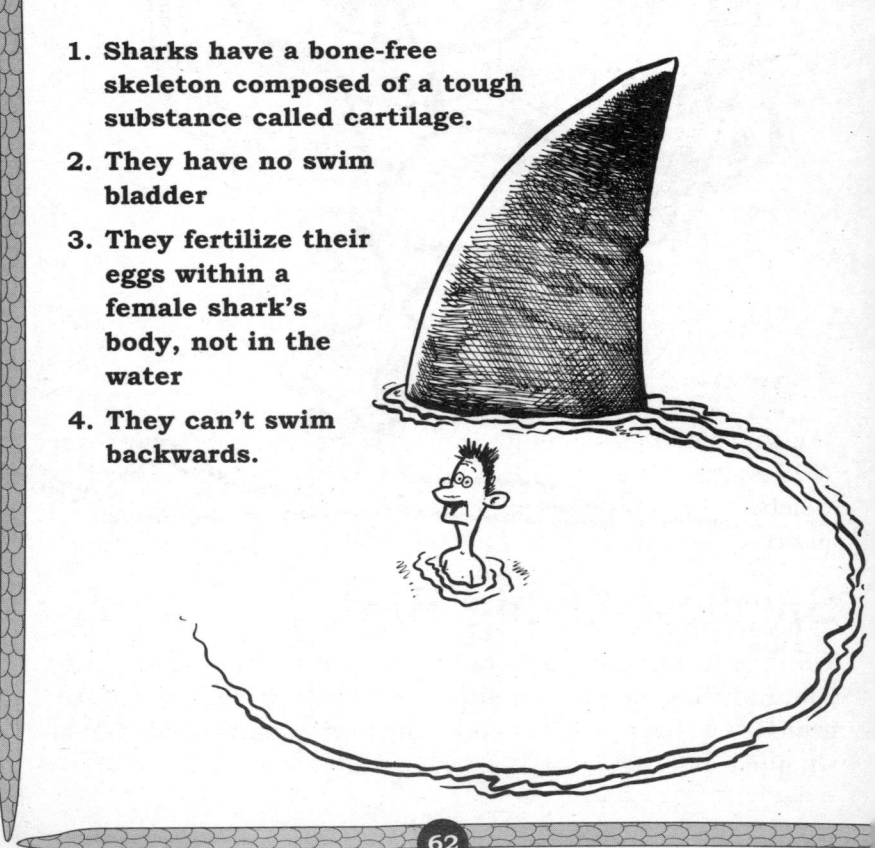

1. **Sharks have a bone-free skeleton composed of a tough substance called cartilage.**
2. **They have no swim bladder**
3. **They fertilize their eggs within a female shark's body, not in the water**
4. **They can't swim backwards.**

# Longest Snake

South-East Asia's reticulated python regularly grows over 6.25 metres in length. In 1912, a python was captured in Celebes, Indonesia, which reached a record length of 10 metres – longer than an old-fashioned double-decker bus.

# Heaviest Flying Bird

The great bustard is both the largest land bird in Europe and the world's heaviest flying bird. A male weighs around 20 kilograms, reaches 105 centimetres in height and has a 2.4-metre wingspan.

# 8. Working Animals

**Whether they are treading the boards or out in a war zone, animals seem to be a lot cleverer than we think – but are you as clever? Can you Find The Fib amongst these facts?**

You may have seen *Babe*, the film featuring the adventures of a pig, raised by sheepdogs, who learns to herd sheep. Well, Babe wasn't just a single clever animal actor. Babe was actually played by a total of 48 real Yorkshire pigs, plus an animatronic double. This was because baby pigs grow so fast. A make-up artist had to put a wig and false eyelashes on a pig for each scene. Then a computer whizz-kid made it seem like all the animals could actually talk.

In the film *The Wizard of Oz*, Toto the dog received 125 dollars a week . . . much more than the actors who played the Munchkins, who were paid a mean 50 dollars a week.

**Oldest Chimp**

The chimp who played Cheeta in the original *Tarzan* movies of the 1930s and 40s was officially named the oldest chimp in the world in 2003. Now, at the ripe old age of 72, Cheeta is still fond of getting a burger and Coke from his local Hollywood drive-in. He also enjoys painting 'ape-stract' pictures, which raise money for unwanted showbiz animals.

In his acting life, Cheeta starred in 12 early *Tarzan* movies. His last role, before retiring to the lap of luxury, was in the 1967 version of *Doctor Doolittle*.

# Animal Names of NAFL American Football Teams:

**Arkansas Rhinos**
**Asheville Grizzlies**
**Bay Atlantic Sharks**
**Central Penn Piranhas**
**Hamilton Screaming Eagles**
**New York Panthers**
**Waco Wolves**
**Willingboro Bears**

American President George W. Bush jumped at the chance to provide one of the voices for the animals in Eddie Murphy's 1998 movie, *Doctor Doolittle*. The president provided the voice for 'Ritzo the Rat', and he had to say 'Aww, c'mon, Doc . . . If you ain't eatin' that hot dog, why not share it round a little, huh?' The actual recording session lasted 2 hours 37 minutes as the president kept forgetting his line.

# Animal Names of American Baseball Teams

**Arizona Diamondbacks**
**Chicago Cubs**
**Detroit Tigers**
**St Louis Cardinals**
**Tampa Bay Devil Rays**

## Bravest Animals

The Dickin Medal is the animal world's version of the Victoria Cross, and marks special acts of animal bravery. During the 1939–45 wartime period, 32 pigeons, 18 dogs, 3 horses and 1 cat won the medal for 'displaying conspicuous gallantry and devotion to duty while serving with the armed forces or civil defence units'.

Three Dickin Medals were awarded following the tragedy of the 9/11 Twin Towers attack. Two medals were awarded to guide dogs, Salty and Roselle, who bravely led their owners to safety, down more than 70 floors of the World Trade Center. To recognize the heroic efforts of the 300 Search and Rescue dogs that worked in the ruins following the terrorist attacks on New York and Washington, a third Dickin Medal was awarded to a German shepherd named Apollo.

In the Second World War, the Germans used dogs to carry messages back from the front. So, what did those plucky Brits do? Did they:
**a)** train the British dogs to drive tanks?
**b)** parachute in packages of poisoned dog food?
**c)** release a female dog in heat?

America's spying agency, the CIA, operated on a cat and turned its tail into a radio antenna so that the cat could act as an animal eavesdropping device. Unfortunately, the cat was run over by a taxi and the Americans had to bring 'Operation Acoustic Kitty' to an abrupt end.

*The answer's c) – Allied troops simply released a female dog in heat, and she returned with a dozen German army dogs following her every paw-step!*

# Mike the Headless Chicken

When Colorado farmer Lloyd Olsen chopped off Mike the Chicken's head in 1945, little did he realize what a huge star his decapitated dinner meal would become. Saved from bleeding to death by a lucky blood clot, the axe blow had obviously left Mike unable to see or cluck, but he could still hear and think. The headless rooster lived on for 18 months, and actually gained weight when taken on tour around America. Customers paid 25 cents to gawp at the beheaded bird, and this earned lucky Lloyd 4,500 dollars a month. Farmer Olsen used a little dropper to drip food and water directly into the chicken's neck. One night in a motel, Mike sadly choked to death when the farmer misplaced the dropper and couldn't clear Mike's airway.

# Eight Space-flight Animals:

1. Yorick the monkey, who made the first successful 'near space' flight in 1951
2. Mildred and Albert — mice used to test weightlessness in 1952
4. Laika the Russian dog, who became the first animal in orbit in 1957
5. Gordo the squirrel monkey travelled over 2,400 kilometres in a 1958 Jupiter rocket
6. Ham the chimp, who proved in 1961 that tasks could be done during launch
7. Felix the cat was launched by the French into space in 1963
8. Arabella the spider who, in 1973, wove her web for the first time in space.

Other animals in space include harvester ants, Japanese tree frogs, a newt, an oyster toadfish, a tortoise and fruit flies (which were, in fact, the first animals in space).

Keiko the killer whale was better known as Willy, star of the *Free Willy* movies. The six-tonne mammal starred in three *Free Willy* movies, in which sympathetic humans help set free a killer whale, long-held captive. Keiko's life began to mirror his character's, but with a much sadder ending. A multi-million-dollar campaign tried to coax him back to the open sea and life with a pod of real killer whales. But in December 2003 Keiko died of pneumonia in the seas off Norway. The name 'Keiko' means 'Lucky One' in Japanese.

Leo the Lion is seen in every MGM feature film shown in the cinema – that's because he's the lion who roars just before the film begins. Leo's film career began in 1928, when his roar was played into cinemas on a record player because all films at that time were silent.

# 9. Baby Animals

'Aww . . . What a lovely baby. And what a lickle, ickle hairy face . . . Mummy's cuddly wuddly baby wart-hog!' You thought your parents were strange? Check out what goes on when babies are born in the animal kingdom. And don't forget to Find That Fib!

The female digger wasp makes a burrow, then goes hunting for long-horned grasshoppers. When she catches them, she merely paralyses them, before sticking them in the burrow, laying her eggs on top. Then she seals up the burrow, leaving her larvae to hatch and enjoy their first tasty meal.

The sea horse is the only male fish that gives birth to its young. The female deposits her eggs in a pouch on the male's underbelly and – once fertilized – the proud father carries those eggs for around 3 weeks before releasing the baby sea horses from his pouch.

The baby cuckoo gives a whole new meaning to the term 'sibling rivalry'. Within an hour of hatching, this oversized fledgling starts working to push the other eggs out of the nest. This nasty trick ensures that baby cuckoo gets all the food, and it soon grows several times larger than the puzzled parent birds feeding it. Incidentally, only males make the traditional 'coo coo' sound – females give a 'bubbling' call.

When the largest marsupial mammal – the red kangaroo – gives birth, her baby is only 2.5 centimetres long and weighs 0.75 grams. It quickly crawls up into its mother's pouch where it stays for safety.

The question is, what do we call a baby kangaroo at birth? Is it:
**a)** Beverley
**b)** Joey
**c)** Stanley

*The answer's b) Joey...And it would take 36,000 baby Joeys to equal the weight of the proud mother kangaroo!*

In the wild, a male giant panda weighs around 85 to 125 kilograms, and female giant pandas weigh between 70 and 100 kilograms. Despite such hefty parents, at birth a panda cub weighs only 100 to 200 grams, and is only 15–17 centimetres long.

Giant pandas have twins almost 50 per cent of the time they give birth; sadly, in the wild they often reject one baby, leaving it to die.

# Baby Names:

A baby bat is called a 'pup'
A baby beaver is called a 'kit'
A baby eel is called an 'elver'
A baby elephant is called a 'calf'
A baby elephant seal is called a 'weaner'
And a baby grouse is called a 'cheeper'.

In remote islands of the Caribbean, the crimson-coloured babyface beetle makes a sound like a baby's rattle as it flies, owing to its habit of rasping its small sets of wings together. Island women catch these beetles and tie them to a piece of string so that they can swing the poor trapped insects over their stomachs – to ensure that they give birth to baby boys!

Here's the normal way different amphibians grow up: either egg to larva (tadpole) to adult (frog or toad); or egg to larva (eft) to adult (newt or salamander).

The axolotl, however, is strange – it's a salamander that never grows up, a bit like the Peter Pan of the world of amphibians. The axolotl prefers to stay in its 'baby' form – complete with feathery gills – and never grows up into a salamander. Keeping its larval feathery gills, it does, however, grow much bigger than it ever would, had it turned into a salamander.

**Youngest Amphibian**

'Mum, are we there yet?'

While we're on the subject of amphibians, the paradoxical frog from the Amazon and Trinidad also doesn't behave normally at birth. The tadpole grows and grow to almost 25 centimetres long – which is four times bigger than the adult frog. No wonder this odd amphibian is also known as the shrinking frog!

Our flat friends, the Suriname toads, seem to give birth from their backs. During mating, the female releases eggs, which (helped by the movements of the male) sink down into the skin of the female's back. Over several days, the eggs will form 'honeycombs' and tadpoles will grow inside these pockets, eventually popping out from their mother's back as fully developed froglets.

Unlike most animals, emperor penguins breed in bitterly cold Antarctic winters, with a female attracting her male by singing a song that only her particular partner will recognize. After the eggs are laid, however, the female seems to lose all interest. She goes off on a two-month feeding spree, leaving the poor male to balance a single cricket ball-sized egg on his feet.

'I've never been good at playing Keepie-Uppie!'

# 10.
# Strange but True

By now, your brain will probably be bursting with all sorts of odd facts; at risk of adding to your problems, here are some more things you never knew you never knew . . . bits of trivia that didn't seem to fit in anywhere else in this book! But can you Find where That Fib fits?

## Four Animals that Seem to Smile All the Time:

### 1. Three-toed sloth:
their mouths are naturally smiley-shaped

### 2. Hyena:
their high cackling laugh is often a sign of fear or intense excitement

### 3. Sea Otter:
while eating, sea otters grin so they don't get spiked by urchin spines

### 4. Dolphins:
are extremely intelligent – no wonder they always look so happy – they're probably thinking how dopey we humans look!

Here's a world record that I wouldn't recommend trying to beat. Texan Jackie Bibby tried to break the world record for juggling jellyfish. He did it, too... keeping seven jellyfish in the air for three minutes. Unfortunately, he was stung so badly in the record-breaking attempt, he had to spend the next month in hospital.

The most common bat in Britain is also its smallest. The pipistrelle bat weighs just 3–8 grams and will fit neatly into a walnut shell.

On one night flight, it can eat up to:

**a)** 12 chicken vindaloo curries and chips
**b)** 3,000 insects
**c)** 5 pizzas (with no anchovies!).

*The answer, of course, is (b)*

# Twelve Animals Associated with Wrestling Terms:

1. Boston crab
2. Bulldog
3. Camel clutch
4. Frog splash
5. Flying mare
6. Gorilla press
7. Gator buster
8. Monkey flip
9. Lion-tamer
10. Spinning cobra clutch
11. Tiger driver
12. Swan dive

The American bison is the largest land animal in North America. Early settlers called them 'buffalo', and nowadays 'buffalo' and 'bison' are used interchangeably. Confusingly, however, the true buffalo of Africa and Asia, like the water buffalo, don't have a humped back, yet they have longer horns than their North American cousins. That's why scientists maintain that buffalo and bison are two different types of animal. Personally, I reckon that the only difference between a buffalo and a bison is . . . you can't wash your hands in a buffalo! (Gettit?)

## Odd Couples

When two different animals live together and help one another to survive, scientists call the process 'symbiosis'. Here are some examples:

**Bustard and carmine bee-eaters:** both are birds – bee-eaters eat insects buzzing around the bustard's head.
**Anemone fish and Sea anemone:** protective mucus on the fish stops anemone stings penetrating their skin.
**Baboons and Impalas:** often move together across the plains, watching out for predators.
**Cleaner shrimps and Moray eels:** shrimps remove skin parasites from the vicious moray eel.
**Egyptian plover and Crocodile:** the plover bird hops inside

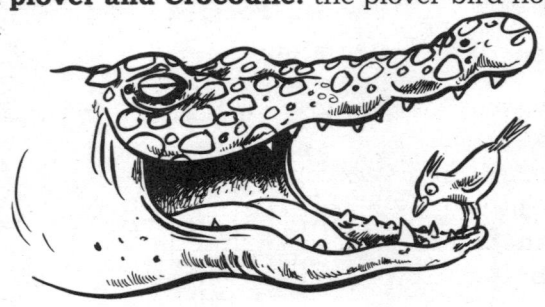

'OK, kids... bone up on this!'

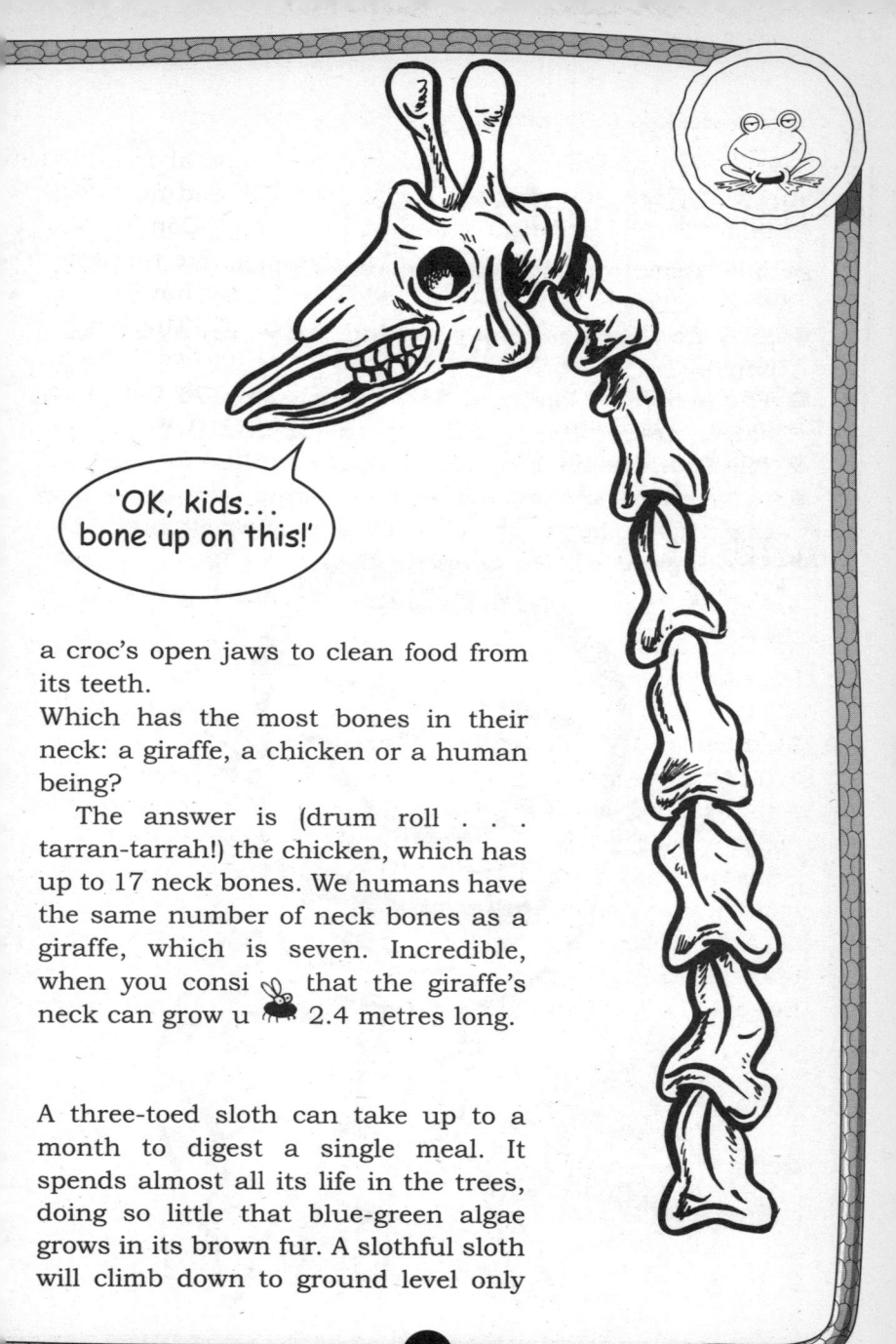

a croc's open jaws to clean food from its teeth.

Which has the most bones in their neck: a giraffe, a chicken or a human being?

The answer is (drum roll . . . tarran-tarrah!) the chicken, which has up to 17 neck bones. We humans have the same number of neck bones as a giraffe, which is seven. Incredible, when you consider that the giraffe's neck can grow up to 2.4 metres long.

A three-toed sloth can take up to a month to digest a single meal. It spends almost all its life in the trees, doing so little that blue-green algae grows in its brown fur. A slothful sloth will climb down to ground level only once a week – and that's only to have a poo!

# Insect Snacks

Eating insects provides a normal diet in Eastern countries.

- **Filipino farmers enjoy eating mole crickets for a snack.**
- **The people of Thailand find a rich source of protein in eating dragonflies, beetle larvae and crickets.**
- **The Chinese eat bee larvae – either boiled or fried.**
- **In Thailand, if chefs can't find a lemon to squeeze over their food, they make do with a juicy black ant.**
- **The Japanese cook grasshoppers in soy sauce to make a sort of . . . well, soy-sauce-flavoured grasshopper crisp.**

*Tastiest Snacks*

# Which Chinese Animal Year Were You Born In?

Find out whether you, your friends and family bear the characteristics of the animal that rules your birth year in this Chinese astrology calendar:

Year of the:

**Monkey** (playful, inventive): 1920, 1932, 1944, 1956, 1968, 1980, 1992, 2004
**Rooster** (courageous, resourceful): 1921, 1933, 1945, 1957, 1969, 1981, 1993, 2005
**Dog** (independent, original, truthful): 1922, 1934, 1946, 1958, 1970, 1982, 1994, 2006
**Pig** or **Boar** (gallant, sincere): 1923, 1935, 1947, 1959, 1971, 1983, 1995, 2007
**Rat** (charming, popular): 1924, 1936, 1948, 1960, 1972, 1984, 1996, 2008
**Ox** (patient, careful, intelligent): 1925, 1937, 1949, 1961, 1973, 1985, 1997, 2009
**Tiger** (dynamic, magnetic): 1926, 1938, 1950, 1962, 1974, 1986, 1998, 2010
**Rabbit** (talented, virtuous, successful): 1927, 1939, 1951, 1963, 1975, 1987, 1999, 2011
**Dragon** (powerful, vital): 1928, 1940, 1952, 1964, 1976, 1988, 2000, 2012
**Snake** (clever, alluring, wise): 1929, 1941, 1953, 1965, 1977, 1989, 2001, 2013
**Horse** (outgoing, spirited): 1930, 1942, 1954, 1966, 1978, 1990, 2002, 2014
**Goat** (successful, good-natured): 1931, 1943, 1955, 1967, 1979, 1991, 2003, 2015

# The Chicken or the Egg

In 2003, an American reporter decided to find out once and for all which came first – the chicken or the egg. She went to a post office in Cambridge, Massachusetts, and posted two packages to a New York City post office, one containing a live chicken and the other containing an egg. The reporter then travelled to that same post office (320 kilometres away) and waited there until both items arrived. Two days later, the chicken arrived. The egg arrived 11 hours later.

# Nutty Names

If a scientist discovers a new species of animal, he or she can choose its scientific name. There are some familiar-sounding species out there. Can you guess who the following are named after?

**'Bufonaria borisbeckeri':** a marine snail, named after Wimbledon tennis champion Boris Becker.
**'Masiakasaurus knopfleri':** a dinosaur, named after Dire Straits rocker Mark Knopfler by Madagascan scientists who liked rock music as much as they liked digging into rocks.
**'Anopthalmus hitleri':** a Slovenian scientist named a blind cave beetle after infamous dictator Adolf Hitler.
**'Polemistus chewbacca':** some *Stars Wars*-loving biologists named a wasp after everyone's favourite Wookiee!

Here are some examples, gathered from the world's zoos and museums, of animals living to extreme old age:

## MAMMALS  YEARS

| | |
|---|---|
| Elephant | 69 |
| Horse | 50 |
| Hippopotamus | 49 |
| Chimpanzee | 40 |
| Grizzly bear | 32 |
| Bison | 30 |
| Lion | 30 |
| Tiger | 25 |
| Elk | 22 |
| Mountain lion | 20 |
| Beaver | 19 |
| Wolf | 16 |
| Squirrel | 16 |

## BIRDS  YEARS

| | |
|---|---|
| Turkey buzzard | 118 |
| Swan | 102 |
| Parrot | 80 |
| Great horned owl | 68 |
| Eagle | 55 |
| Sparrow | 23 |
| Canary | 22 |
| Hummingbird | 8 |

## REPTILES YEARS

| | |
|---|---|
| Giant tortoise | 152 |
| Box turtle | 123 |
| Alligator | 68 |
| Snapping turtle | 57 |
| Cobra | 28 |

# It's raining... Catfish/Dogfish?

Back in 1918, the residents of Sunderland, in north-east England, must have been surprised when several hundred sand eels poured down in heavy rain from the skies.

This wasn't just a weird one-off. On the morning of 9 February 1859, the inhabitants of Aberdare, Wales, were subjected to a shower of sticklebacks. It seems that in both cases a small but powerful tornado formed above the surface of the water. Acting like a giant vacuum cleaner, the wind sucked up the fish and eels into the air. As the wind died down, it sent the fishy passengers spraying down with the rain.

# 11. Bird Brains

**Our feathered friends are the subject of this next selection of fantastic facts which are about as easy to digest as a sparrow attempting to swallow an anaconda! Now let's see you fly off and Find That Fib amongst these feathered facts!**

Insects, frogs, lizards and even mice that get caught by a hungry red-backed shrike end up suffering the grisliest of deaths – they get skewered, then left in what serves for a bird larder. The busy shrike grabs its prey in its beak and impales the unfortunate victim on a handy spike sticking out of a thorn bush, or on a length of barbed wire. Yuck!

# Top Five Strange Names for Pigeons:

**5. White Jacobin**
**4. Yellow Danish Tumbler**
**3. Old Dutch Capuchine**
**2. Budapester Short-Face Tumbler**
**1. Black-Laced Blondinette**

The strangely-named Kakapo or Owl Parrot lives in New Zealand and weighs up to 3.5 kg. However, the Kakapo's flight muscles only account for 3-4% of its total body weight, which makes it too heavy to fly. It spends all its nights looking for food on the ground. By day, it sleeps in holes under rocks or trees. It is now the world's rarest parrot, with only approximately 62 of the birds left.

# Colourful Types of Hummingbird:

Black-chinned
Blue-headed
Bronze-tailed
Copper-rumped
Green-breasted
Indigo-capped
Olive-spotted
Purple-throated
Ruby-topaz
Sapphire-bellied
Shining-green
Spot-throated
Violet-chested
White-eared

Percy, a confused and short-sighted grey heron that used to visit Whitby Safari Park in Yorkshire, once tried to attack a black-and-white striped Mini Cooper car. It had mistaken the Mini for its deadly enemy: the white tiger!

'Think I need a close shave this Christmas...'

Wild turkeys are known to grow beards. These can be from a few centimetres in length, up to more than 30 centimetres. They range in colour from dark grey to black. Some turkeys never grow one, while others grow a number of beards, just to make up! The beard is composed of bristle-like feathers that emerge from one follicle (that's the tube holding a feather in place). Sometimes ice and snow can build up on the tip of the turkey's beard, causing it to become brittle and break off!

# Combs for Chicks

The floppy flaps of flesh on the top of a chicken's head are called combs. The combs are usually red in colour, but some breeds have purple combs.

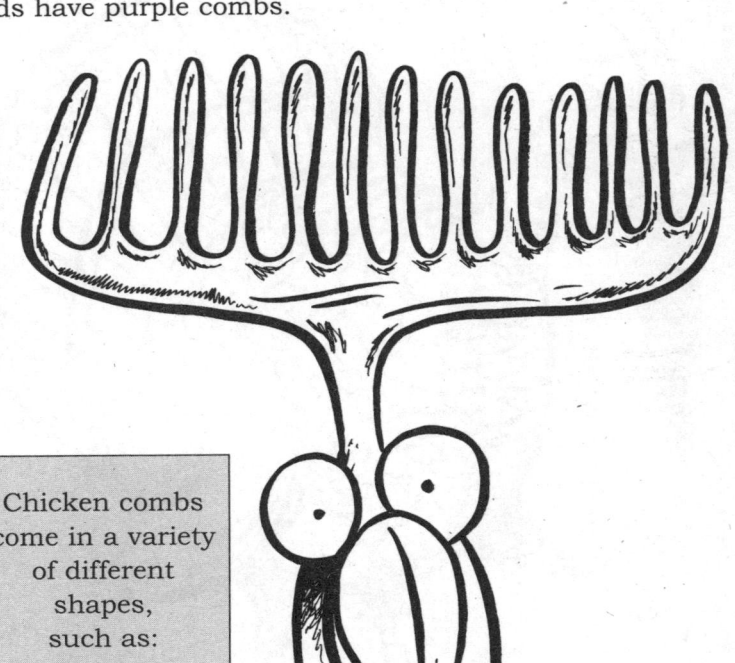

Chicken combs come in a variety of different shapes, such as:

**Pea**
**Buttercup**
**V-shaped**
**Cushion**
**Single**
**Rose**
**Walnut**
**Strawberry**

Although flamingos are very elegant creatures, they do have some odd habits. For a start, they like standing on one leg. They have to turn their beaks upside down underwater to eat. They then swish the bulky beaks back and forth to filter out tasty bits of algae from the lake water. Eating this algae, plus small insects and crustaceans, provides the protein to turn their feathers pink.

Hummingbirds are the only birds able to fly in reverse – a trick they perform because they have to dip in and out of flowers. They do this using a special rotating joint which allows these tiny yet muscle-packed birds to beat their wings in a figure-of-eight motion. Their wings beat at anything from 22 to 78 times per second, and sometimes up to an incredible 200 beats per second – when a male hummingbird is trying to impress the ladies!

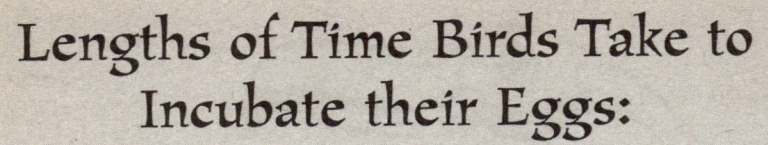

# Lengths of Time Birds Take to Incubate their Eggs:

**Chicken – 21 days**
**Turkey – 28 days**
**Muscovy duck – 35–37 days**
**Goose – 28–34 days**
**Guinea fowl – 28 days**
**Pheasant – 23–28 days**
**Grouse – 25 days**
**Ostrich – 42 days**

**And the winner is...**
**Emu**
**– which takes**
**a whopping**
**52 days.**

Biologists have studied intelligence among animals and found that birds are brighter than chimpanzees or dolphins. When it comes to using tools to perform tough tasks, a finch may have a brain the size of a peppercorn, but it's still brighter than a chimp, whose brain weighs 500 grams.

## Animals that Glide
### (other than birds):

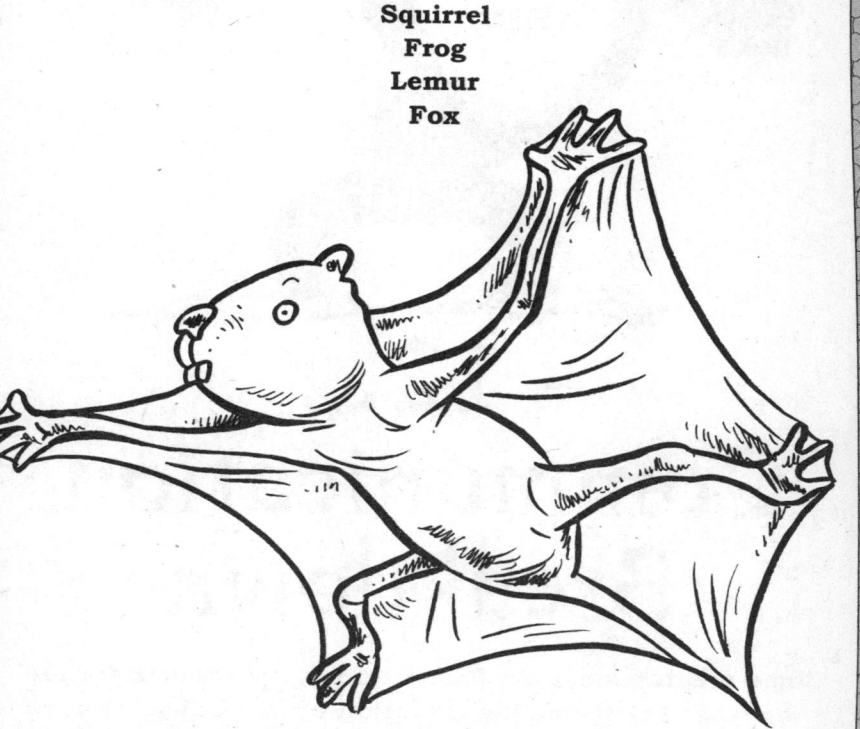

**Squirrel**
**Frog**
**Lemur**
**Fox**

Flying Lemurs aren't actually related to the monkey family's lemurs. However, they can glide distances of 100 metres, making it seem like they can fly.

# 12.
# Communication Breakdown

Some creatures can do flashy things – particularly when they want to attract the attention of the ladies, or warn their mates about a passing hunter. Whether it's a trick with the throat or a click of their beak, it's always impressive . . . almost as impressive as Finding That Fib!

The hippopotamus whirls its tail round like a helicopter when it's doing a poo.

This extreme action spreads the poo all over the place, including up into the trees and bushes. In doing so, the hippo:
**a)** is a social pariah
**b)** is marking his or her territory
**c)** is suffering from the effects of eating too much fruit.

'Funny thing is, I'm still a fan of that hippo!'

### Messiest Poo

*The answer's b) But who would want a territory covered in poo?*

# Three Animals that Can Blow Out Their Throats Like Massive Balloons:

**1.** The frigate bird
**2.** The European tree frog
**3.** Kirtland's tree snake

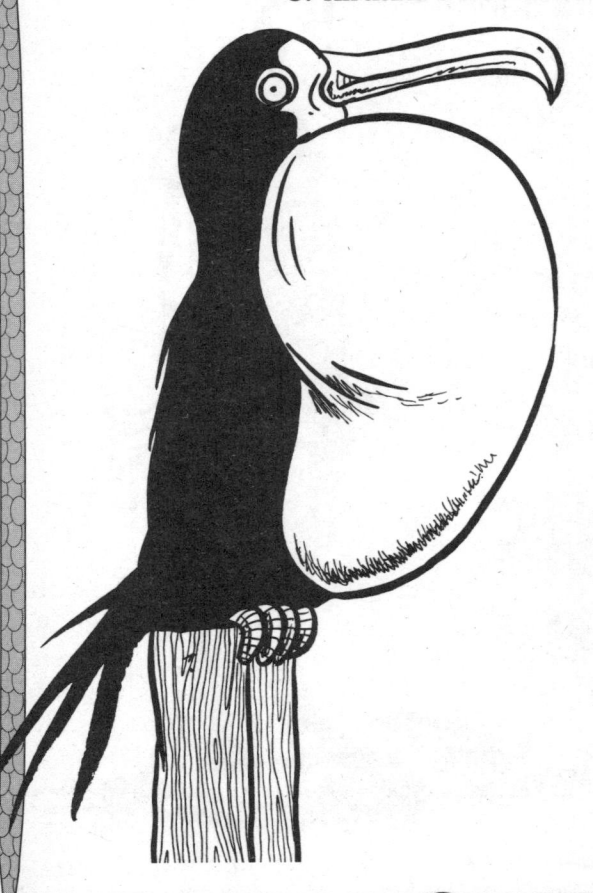

The male kingfisher sings a rather strange bird-call during the breeding season. The kingfisher throws its head back to attract females and makes a rapid clacking noise by vibrating a flap in the back of his throat. Birdwatchers are convinced that the resulting yodel-like mating call sounds as if the kingfisher's saying, 'Go and turn the telly on! Go and turn the telly on!'

# Barmy Bird Calls

Birds don't sing distinctive songs just to communicate with one another, however. Coots make a distinctive sound by stamping. Frigate birds, storks and albatrosses clack their beaks together. Mute swans and wood pigeons make sounds by flapping their wings, and woodpeckers rat-a-tat on hollow tree trunks. However, no one can beat the palm cockatoo for strange sounds. During courtship, this barmy bird makes drumsticks out of twigs and whacks them against a hollow log whilst dancing a pirouette.

Sperm whales communicate with each other using a system of clicks – like in Morse code – known as a 'coda'.

They often begin conversations with a five-click coda, which is their way of saying, 'Hello'.

Bull sperm whales make a 'clang' or 'big click'. Repeated every seven seconds, this sounds like a heavy jail door being clanged shut. Does this impress the ladies? Or scare away other male whales? How should I know? I'm not a sperm whale . . .

The male firefly emits a pattern of light flashes as it dashes around, trying to attract a female. A female firefly responds with a different flash pattern, and the male dashes over to mate. For example, the male photinus firefly makes two flashes, two seconds apart. The female photinus firefly replies one second later with a single flash.

These incendiary insects have to be careful, though. The nasty, cannibal-like photinus firefly copies the photinus female's flashing pattern, and when the photinus male falls for its mimicking and flies in to mate, it ends up being eaten by the greedy photinus firefly!

'I hope those flashy fellers don't realize I need a light snack!'

Elephants talk in a broad range of frequencies. They make sounds as low as the lowest note on a grand piano, and as high as the top note of a clarinet.

But what do the females of the species sound like? Is it like:
**a)** your teacher throwing a wobbler?
**b)** all the car alarms in your street going off at once?
**c)** a jackhammer?

*The answer's c). Female African elephants looking for mates can rumble as loud as a jackhammer. The resulting racket can reach the flapping ears of eager males over a range of more than 175 kilometres.*

# 13. Our Furry Friends

Time for one final round of fabulously fascinating facts. These are the sort of facts that can make the fur fly, as family and friends argue, bicker and disbelieve you while you display your superior general knowledge. See, you really do know best. You also know which one of this selection is an out-and-out lie – or do you? Go on ... Find That Fib!

The huge ears of the Californian leaf-nosed bat help it to earn its other name: the 'whispering bat'. Through its nose it sends out high-frequency sounds by contracting muscles in its windpipe. It then picks up sound waves bouncing off its prey. This is such an accurate procedure that the whispering bat can detect objects as fine as a human hair.

American scientists have apparently trained rats to sniff out humans trapped under the rubble of collapsed buildings. These animal agents are fitted with a tiny 'radio backpack' that connects with the rat's brain. The rescue rats use their keen sense of smell to recognize human scent and then give out a brain signal. This is picked up by a radio transmitter and leads rescuers to the trapped person.

Sea otters have an amazing 100,000 hairs per square centimetre of skin. That's more per centimetre than us humans have on our entire heads... not including your Uncle Doug, who's bald!.

'I'm not bald! I just have a big head!'

**Top Three Most Boring Meals in the Animal Kingdom**

**3.** The blue whale which daily eats up to 4 tonnes of shrimp-like creatures called krill. It does this every day for about 120 days.

**2.** The giant panda, which eats between 10 and 18 kg of bamboo shoots and leaves every day. This makes up 99 per cent of its diet – the remainder is made up of other plants and meat.

**1.** The koala, which lives entirely in eucalyptus trees, and therefore eats about 1 kilogram of eucalyptus leaves every day. It would be quite helpless on the ground.

Gerbils were trained as customs guards by the Israeli security forces because the small rodents have a strong sense of smell. The hope was that the gerbils would be able to sniff out nervous aeroplane hijackers who were sweating buckets. The trouble was, the gerbils were picking out innocent travellers who were just scared of flying.

'Go on, boy. Sniff 'em out!'

I hope I don't get this wrong!

In 2001, MI5 – the UK's spying agency – also revealed that it had planned to use gerbils as secret agents, with a mission to seek out Russian spies during the cold war. It gave up the idea when the gerbils didn't spot many spies at all.

When a Norwegian lemming digs out a tunnel, its skin is so loose that it can turn round inside its own skin. Oh, and one more thing about lemmings: they don't commit mass suicide by jumping off cliffs. It's just a mass migration or movement of lemmings that led to the myth.

When it starts to feel hungry, the sea otter is a clever creature. It makes a meal out of a spiny sea urchin by first wrapping seaweed strands round the urchin's round shell. Hey presto! The seaweed breaks off any poisonous prickly bits.

What else does the otter do that's impressive? Does it:
**a)** ride a bicycle whilst juggling starfish?
**b)** crack open mussel shells on its tummy?
**c)** sing the French national anthem every night before bedtime?

*The answer's b). That's not the sea otter's only teatime trick. While floating on its back in the Pacific Ocean, the otter also likes to crack open mussel shells by whacking them hard against a stone which it balances on its tummy.*

## Biggest Family

Black-tailed prairie dogs dig massive networks of tunnels and burrows underneath the North American grasslands. One 'town' – as prairie dog colonies are called – was discovered in 1904 and was thought to stretch 160 x 380 kilometres in area. It was home to around 400 million individuals.

For years, people have thought that the word 'kangaroo' comes from Captain James Cook chatting with an Aborigine in 1770. Cook had landed on the north-east coast of Australia, spotted several kangaroos bouncing past and asked what those creatures were called. The local Aborigine replied, 'Kangaroo,' meaning, 'I don't know,' and the name stuck. Recently, however, language experts have found the word '*gangurru*' is actually an ancient Aboriginal word for 'kangaroo'.

Don't ever offer a male lion an orange, or a melon, or any type of fruit – it won't eat it. The male lion restricts its diet to red meat because it's learnt that its mane falls out after eating fruit. A scientific study of lion prides in the Serengeti showed that a vegetarian diet amongst male lions does cause premature hair loss – and male lions do love their magnificent manes!

In August 2004, a rabbit was hiding in a bonfire at Devizes Cricket Club, Wiltshire. When the bonfire was lit, it was a case of 'Run, Rabbit, Run', as it escaped with its tail alight. It took shelter nearby and set a shed on fire, causing £60,000 worth of damage! Eleven firefighters were unable to save the shed or its contents. That was one hot, cross bunny . . . and the cricket club weren't too pleased, either!

# 14. Find That Fib...Answers

## Chapter 1. Creepy Crawlies
If you thought the story about the soft-drink-sucking mosquitoes having a thirst for fizzy drinks instead of blood was pure balderdash, then Congratulations! You Found That Fib!

However, did you know that – in real life – it's only the female mosquitoes that like to suck our blood, and they transmit malaria as they do so. Male mosquitoes actually prefer slurping plant juice and sweet nectar.

## Chapter 2. Under the Water
If you thought there was something fishy about a goldfish being coloured yellowy-green and not orange, then – Congratulations! You Found That Fib!

However, it's actually true that goldfish do lose their colour if they are kept in a dim light, or in running water, such as a stream.

## Chapter 3. Dangerous Animals!
If you thought that story about surfers preventing box jellyfish stings by wearing silk pyjamas was a load of tosh, then Congratulations! You Found That Fib!

However, Australian surfers – who really are bothered by box jellyfish stings – have found they can prevent any painful stings simply by wearing ladies' tights or stockings over their arms and legs.

## Chapter 4. Down in the Jungle

If you thought the square-lipped rhino fact was far-fetched, then Congratulations – You Found That Fib!

Sadly, all rhinos are on the brink of extinction. The square-lipped white rhino is one of only five species or types of rhinoceros alive today. The others are:

Asian one-horned rhino
Black rhino
Javan rhino
Sumatran rhino.

## Chapter 5. Masters of Disguise

If you didn't believe that a Cinderella caterpillar could pretend to be a deadly spider in order to chase away hungry eagles, then Congratulations! You Found That Fib!

However, in real life the tiny Madagascan butterfly caterpillar can perform a similar trick and easily terrify much bigger baboons. It does this by inflating its rear end so that it looks like the spitting image of a snake's head, complete with scale-like markings and horrible beady eyes! The cunning caterpillar then sways like a deadly snake to complete the illusion, and this scares off would-be monkey hunters . . . Whoah, scary!

## Chapter 6. Incredible Journeys

If you reckoned that the story about a chimpanzee called Dumbo having big ears was pure nonsense, then Congratulations! You Found That Fib, and your own ears must be burning!

However, it is a fact that some animals really do have excellent hearing – and, my, what big ears the fennec fox has got! They're so big, in fact, that the fennec can hear another animal moving even if it's 1,500 metres away.

## Chapter 7. Record-breaking Birds and Beasts

Congratulations if you reckoned that the whopping great mammoth dragonfly – an insect that often had a heart attack when it flapped its wings – didn't actually exist at all. You found an equally whopping great fib!

However, the record for the world's heaviest insect is actually held by the endangered giant weta of Little Barrier Island, New Zealand – one specimen having reached a maximum weight of 71 grams – easily heavier than a regulation tennis ball!

## Chapter 8. Working Animals

If you guessed that there's no way the president of the United States of America would play the voice of a rat in the Eddie Murphy movie *Doctor Doolittle*, then go to the head of the class! You Found That Fib!

However, one of the many celebrities who really do provide a voice for an animal in that same film – that of a female pigeon – is actress Julie Kavner . . . though you know her better as the voice of everyone's favourite cartoon mom, Marge Simpson.

## Chapter 9. Baby Animals

If you disbelieved the tale about women whirling a babyface beetle over their stomachs to guarantee having a baby boy, then you Found That Fib!

However, a frog known as the African clawed toed (that's 'toed' as in having toes on each foot) was really used as an early type of pregnancy test. Apparently, chemicals in the urine of pregnant women would cause this frog to lay eggs.

## Chapter 10. Strange but True

Texan Jackie Bibby was a real record breaker, but not for juggling jellyfish. That was the Fib! He actually took nine live wriggling western diamond rattlesnakes and stuffed them in his mouth to claim a new world record for... err... a mouthful of rattlesnakes.

## Chapter 11. Bird Brains

If you guessed that Percy the heron attacking a Mini car which he'd mistaken for a white tiger was totally made up, then you Found That Fib!

However, here's a real-life story about a short-sighted bird. Andy, a lonely and confused male Andean flamingo, spent two weeks at a Gloucestershire nature reserve trying to hatch out a pebble which he thought was an egg. Bird experts decided that broody Andy was totally confused because he had been left without a mate at the end of the breeding season.

## Chapter 12. Communication Breakdown

Of course, if you were convinced that the male kingfisher actually yodels, 'Go and turn the telly on! Go and turn the telly on!' as they call for females, then I'm afraid you were taken in by That Fib.

Having said that, however, birdwatchers really are convinced that the yellowhammer sings a song which sounds like it's saying 'a little bit of bread and no cheese'. What's more, it sings the same birdie song more than 3,000 times a day.

## Chapter 13. Our Furry Friends

Congratulations if you reckoned that the story about male lions losing their manes after going on a 'veggie' diet was a bald lie! It was.

However, it is a fact that chimpanzees, South American nakari, and stump-tailed macaque monkeys all show signs of baldness when they become adults. Seems like some dads have more in common with monkeys than they'd care to believe, eh?

## Puffin by Post

## *Know-It-All Guides: Incredible Creatures* – Nigel Crowle

If you have enjoyed this book and want to read more,
then check out these other great Puffin titles.
You can order any of the following books direct with Puffin by Post:

| | |
|---|---|
| *Know-It-All Guides: Conquering Romans* • Nigel Crowle • 0141319775 | £3.99 |
| Fascinating trivia and far-out facts | |

| | |
|---|---|
| *The Time Wreccas* • Val Tyler • 0141318570 | £5.99 |
| An exciting fantasy adventure that takes place in a world within our world | |

| | |
|---|---|
| *Dazzling Discoveries* • Mary and John Gribbin • 0141319720 | £6.99 |
| 'Among the very best'<br>– Phillip Pullman | |

| | |
|---|---|
| *Artemis Fowl: The Opal Deception* • Eoin Colfer • 0141381647 | £12.99 |
| 'Wickedly brilliant'<br>– *Independent* | |

| | |
|---|---|
| *How I Live Now* • Meg Rosoff • 0141318015 | £6.99 |
| 'A crunchily perfect knock-out of a debut novel'<br>– *Guardian* | |

**Just contact:**

Puffin Books, C/o Bookpost, PO Box 29,
Douglas, Isle of Man, IM99 1BQ
Credit cards accepted. For further details:
Telephone: 01624 677237
Fax: 01624 670923

You can email your orders to: bookshop@enterprise.net
Or order online at: www.bookpost.co.uk

**Free delivery in the UK.**
Overseas customers must add £2 per book.

Prices and availability are subject to change.

Visit puffin.co.uk to find out about the latest titles, read extracts and
exclusive author interviews, and enter exciting competitions.
You can also browse thousands of Puffin books online.